I0429515

# BLUE EYES IN THE NEJD

# BLUE EYES IN THE NEJD

Douglas McNary

Copyright © 2014 Douglas McNary
All rights reserved.

ISBN-10: 146999805X
ISBN-13: 9781469998053

This book is dedicated to the memory of Duane McNary, and to all the members of the US and allied militaries who gave their last full measure of devotion in the deserts of Arabia and Southwest Asia.

# Table of Contents

Location of the Nejd in Saudi Arabia, on the Arabian Peninsula

I t is as far from home as a Caucasian Midwesterner can be, both literally and figuratively. Everything about it speaks to a grand contradiction between simplicity and complexity, between brutality and beauty, between mere survival and majestic glory. To the Western mind's eye, it is easier to accept its stereotypes than seek to understand the truly foreign.

"It" is the Nejd, the vast sweep of Arabian desert that is the desolate, fascinating core of the Arabian Peninsula. The Nejd is a love-it-or-hate it place (usually, for outsiders, it's a "hate-it"), a not-so-fickle mistress who seduces from her recline on a sandy, windy furnace. She defines "acquired taste." The acquisition is expensive, and the taste is of salty, warm yogurt ("tastes like camel's milk"). For those who seek to understand the misunderstood, to those whom physical discomfort or barriers do not deter, and who see God's (Allah's) hand in nature's expanse, however, the Nejd is alluring, captivating, and beautiful all in the same breath.

As a military transport descended and landed at Riyadh Air Base and the rear cargo doors opened, I gazed out into the sun and sand and heat of the Nejd. "My God…" was my first and lingering response.

Please take note: I hope you'll find some reading satisfaction in this overly long missive—a memoir of an American in a special place at a unique time. It is a story that may seem dated to well-read Westerners, but "dated" is appropriate to this desert. It is a mere "mark time" in the long march and long memory of Arab history. Issues and conflicts rise and pass, but the Nejd and her immutable characteristics will endure far past our attention spans toward the region.

I was an American military officer stationed in Riyadh and the Nejd during the challenging period of Saudi Arabia in the last half of the 1980s. The oil crises had done their bit, the First Gulf War (Desert Storm) was a ways off, and the Iran-Iraq War was bloodily raging to the north. A fairly small group of Americans flew surveillance and air-refueling aircraft out of Riyadh to guard the skies of the oil-rich Eastern Province of Saudi Arabia.

Some of us would fight Iran in the Gulf actions known to history as Operations Earnest Will and Praying Mantis, during which Kuwaiti crude-oil tankers were reflagged under the US flag so they could be protected by the US military. A mine-laying ship (the *Iran Ajr*) was captured attempting to lay mines in the Northern Gulf, three Iranian-claimed oil and natural gas platforms were demolished by US forces, and there was significant loss of life not only by the Iranians, but also in the tragic mistake that put an Iraqi Exocet anti-ship missile into the *USS Stark*. Later the *USS Vincennes* would shoot down an Iranian Airbus airliner while the commercial jet was flying a distinctly noncommercial flight profile in the southern Gulf. Many of us would go on to fight the Iraqis in Operation Desert Storm.

For the most part, however, our presence was small, and the rare chance to learn about and admire the Nejd was available. That had not always been the case before, and major war would soon completely change the American view of the Nejd, but for that brief period, the desert winds tried to blow wisdom toward those who would genuinely hear it.

Clarity must be stressed on three points. First, I am not a true Arabist. I am a student of the Middle East writ large and an armchair student of Arabic, but "Arabist" is a title reserved for accomplished scholars who speak that wonderful language fluently.

Second, all of this is based on the aforementioned period between the oil crises and Desert Storm. As we will see, the land does not change, but people, on occasion, do alter events. In addition to three major regional wars, the emergence of the Islamic State, the "Arab Spring" toppling of autocratic leaders in the Middle East, Syrian civil war, and even the debate over Arab women and automobiles have proffered change in the region. This is a book about a unique time in history.

Finally, I make no presumption of penning a sweeping history—merely a memoir. For what many consider the definitive book on the history of oil, see Daniel Yergin's *The Prize: The Epic Quest for Oil, Money and Power* (and his recent book on global energy, *The Quest: Energy, Security, and the Remaking of the Modern World*). For history on Saudi Arabia, I recommend Robert Lacey's *The Kingdom: Arabia and the House of Sa'ud* and *Inside the Kingdom: Kings, Clerics, Modernists, Terrorists, and the Struggle for Saudi Arabia*. For a capacious view of Arab history generally, you might see Albert Hourani's *A History of the Arab Peoples*.

With that, I hope you enjoy this modest contribution, and *mysalaama*—go in peace.

Desert "roses" (mineral formations) from an escarpment northwest of Riyadh

# 2

## The Land That Time Remembered

It is an absolute fact: as surely as the day follows the night, as surely as gravity works, the Nejd is 100 percent desert. A real, "I'll kick your ass if you don't respect me" desert—a no-Hollywoodesque-dunes, no-saguaro-cacti, no-belly-dancers desert. It is the wind and sun and sand and little—precious little—water. The rare oases it hosts are few and vital (*riyadh* is Arabic for "spring").

The starkness can be mesmerizing. The very believable story is told of an elderly Bedou standing at the edge of an oasis, hands out, motionless, facing west. When a visitor asked his Arab host what the old man was doing, the response was, "He's breathing in the desert." After decades of tents, camels, sand, and movement, the Nejd still held his heart. Waxing anthropomorphic, it rather seems the Nejd and her sparse populations prefer their independence and only by virtue of rowdy siblings and noisy neighbors became an historic crossroads (or more accurately, a "crossdesert"). In the long run—the only run that counts in Araby—their independence seems assured. That should not discourage a Nejdi walkabout.

I started in Riyadh, the capital of Saudi Arabia, at the Al Yamamah ("The Dove") hotel, a 1960s-era hotel for Americans temporarily assigned to air missions.[1] A pool, a barber, free soda 24/7, absolutely

---

1 You have probably guessed that the name of Al Yamamah was a source of mirth as aircrews and maintenance personnel rotated through. As in, "It's not Al Yamamah, it's yo' mama," etc. Also, as in many Arabic words, the meaning can change with changes in syllabic emphasis.

no bar, and the occasional cat falling through the open hole in the ceiling where the main light fixture should have been. Better accommodations could be had, and I would later stay at the Marriott and—best of all—in a walled compound. But the Al Yamamah was great for a young officer willing to jump on a local bus into the heart of Riyadh.

And so I did, riding down Abdul Aziz Road to the souqs (markets), the historic Mesmark fortress, "Justice Plaza" (many Americans called it "Chop-Chop Square"), and other more workaday malls; black-market music stores; and simply strolling among the *aghal-*, *ghutra-*, and *thobe-* (the circular headband, headscarf, and neck-to-toe white shirt) clad men and *abaya*-wearing women (covered in black, save for the eyes). Some of the Americans called the combination "bowling pins and raisins." Not a recommended diplomatic approach.

More to follow on all of these. But my dinners in Riyadh deserve mention, if not a Zagat rating. Invariably, I stopped for a roadside schwarma, a shaved-meat/yogurt mixture carved to order from a rotating pillar and wrapped in pita-type unleavened bread—and for me, a hot pepper included lengthwise. In the heat of a Riyadh evening, with me the only Westerner in sight, this basic culinary treat was perfect.

There is no tourism in Saudi Arabia (although visas are issued for Islamic worship), so everyone in the bustling souqs was either a Saudi or an expatriate. The latter tended to gather at the New Gold Souq (so named to distinguish it from the Old Gold Souq). On first sight, these particular souqs amaze the Westerner. They are basically open-air stalls of which every square inch is covered with gold. Gold necklaces, bracelets, charms, "her name in Arabic," and on and on. One curious charm in virtually all gold souqs is a necklace from which a totem is hung. That totem, that

---

Another meaning for *al yamamah* is "the toilet." So you can imagine the confusion when, on the way to meet another officer at a Riyadh restaurant, I asked a passing Saudi where "the Toilet Restaurant" was located.

piece of jewelry, is a life-size, blue, faux human eyeball. Arabs, you may note, do not as a rule have blue eyes. The blue eye has thus become a symbol of either great goodness or great evil. It is up to the wearer and Allah to determine which, a lesson I rapidly learned: I have blue eyes.

The open desert around Riyadh is of rather diverse terrain as far as the Nejd goes. Escarpments and low hills are frequent. North of the capital is Dariyah, an oasis retreat previously used by the Al Saud—the Saudi royal family. There is also the occasional ravine, evidence of long-gone water. In certain of the geologic formations within about an hour from Riyadh, the "desert rose" can be uncovered. These are sand compressed over time to form a rose-shaped crystal formation.

Leaving Riyadh and headed due north, we left behind virtually all semblance of geographic diversity. The desert lies flat for hundreds—nay, thousands—of square miles to the border with Iraq and beyond (the Nejd in total within Saudi Arabia is about four hundred thousand square miles). While the area named "the Nejd" is a province of Saudi Arabia, the terrain features continue into southern Iraq and Kuwait. The most commanding height within it is the Wadi al Bateen (*wadi* is Arabic for "creek bed"), which rises up to, oh, ten to twenty feet above desert level. The rest of this northern desert is flat—perhaps the largest flat place in the world. Horizon to horizon, nothing but sand, wind, and sun.

The Nejd continues north into Iraq, where small but hardy vegetation starts to emerge. It ends before the Euphrates River and the ancient Fertile Crescent. On across the Euphrates, the desert also yields to the Ur, also known as the Ur of the Chaldees. It is a structure that many theologians believe was the home of Abraham. You need only read the first chapter of Matthew or Genesis and Exodus in the Christian Bible, or the appropriate passages in Torah or the Koran, to realize the importance of the Ur.

From the northern edge of the Nejd, I turned east, following the Iraqi and Kuwaiti border to the Arabian Gulf. (As an aside, when you see a straight line on a map of the Middle East, it generally means a state boundary determined by someone other than the peoples near those borders. Our British friends usually take the credit for a certain facility in border-drawing.) Astride the Saudi-Kuwaiti border, the aforementioned Wadi al Bateen came into view. My military eye noted the Maginot Line it was not, but rather a dimple in the desert. In another strategic foreshadowing, I recognized the ease with which our four-wheel-drive vehicle coursed over the hard-pan desert. This led me to wonder if an American Abrams tank or Bradley fighting vehicle could pass as easily. Obviously, it turned out they could.

Eventually, the northern Arabian Gulf (in local usage, it's called "Arabian" instead of "Persian") was visible. Reaching the shore, I realized it was a vile sort of overgrown lake, so oily at the surface that from the air, you could see the wake of a crude tanker six hours or more after the ship had passed. I'd also been warned about the Gulf's poisonous sea snakes. Fairly short, with a slim head like a North American coral snake (except it's a sickly green color), the snake's mouth is so small that it can only bite where skin allows it—to wit, between human fingers and toes. I was once told I was seeing them riding the bow wave of a US naval vessel to which I'd been stationed, but their color and the murk of the Gulf made it difficult.

I then headed south along the Gulf coast, definitely leaving the Nejd off to the west. Ahead lay, to use Daniel Yergin's words, "the prize." Oil, oil everywhere, and not a refinery in sight (at the time, the Saudis exported crude but had to import refined products). This is Saudi Arabia's Eastern Province. As I closed on Ad Damman and Dhahran, the Western "footprint" increased, with ARAMCO employees, other oil workers, and the roar of Royal Saudi Air Force (RSAF) American-built F-15s overhead. The island nation of

Bahrain[2] waited at the end of the King Fahd Causeway as I headed farther south, past the small peninsula nation of Qatar.[3]

I continued south, the "Trucial Coast" states of the United Arab Emirates lying to the east. They're called "trucial" due to a maritime truce that eventually placed seven separate states into one country with seven different local governments. Thus, they have one very good airline (Emirates) and one military, but they are known by city-state names. Two of them—Abu Dhabi and Dubai—have the only resorts I know of on the Gulf and are fairly popular with European tourists. While they have ample oil and gas reserves, they have also turned into a global banking and financial center. If you are of an age to remember pre-civil war Beirut, the modern description is often that it's the "Paris (or New York) of the Middle East." But we passed the UAE abeam, leaving the sunscreen and money changing for later as we wheeled to the west, putting Oman at our left shoulders.

That turn to the west led to one of the most forbiddingly brutal places on earth—the *Rub al-Khali*, or "Empty Quarter." It *is* empty, and it makes up about a quarter of Saudi Arabia. It is the world's largest sand desert. Most of its southern flank borders Oman, with a bit next to Yemen. The Rub al-Khali is so beastly, it suffices to say that even camels and survival experts give it a wide berth. Some Iranians insist that the deserts of northeastern Iran are so bad, the area must

---

2 As an aside, at the time the Gulf off Bahrain was the anchorage for the command ship for COMIDEASTFOR (US Navy Commander, Middle East Force), the USS *LaSalle*. Against the Gulf sun, she was painted white and became known as the "Great White Ghost of the Arabian Coast." I was temporarily posted aboard in the wake of the Iraqi Exocet missile attack on the USS *Stark*, and every US ship mounted the Phalanx antimissile gun system against missile attacks. Sailors manned machine guns port and starboard, bow and stern. Near the Bahraini coast, dhows were everywhere. Dhows have not changed appreciably over the centuries, and the contrast between Arab history and Western modernity was striking.

3 Back in the United States, fellow officers and I decided to try to "twin" with an Arab town. We picked Umm Bob in Qatar (our soccer team was "The Umm Bob Rockin' Roberts"). I got to see Umm Bob for myself, and if I may say so, we picked the wrong place—unless one prefers saltwater marshes and record humidity.

be Allah's (bless his holy name) waste bin. That may be true—but if so, the Rub al-Khali is His whole garbage truck.

Thankfully, the desert yields to greenery as the land rises to a rather nice coastline. The Red Sea was strikingly beautiful and almost crystalline as I traveled north, enjoying the view. This coast is popular even with Americans living in Saudi Arabia. The sights seen by scuba divers or snorkelers in the Red Sea were remarkable given the water's clarity and the abundance of marine life as we headed toward Mecca and Medina. (The infidel's temptation to visit Mecca and the Grand Mosque in the holiest site in Islam should be avoided—it is not allowed, and they are serious.) Ahead lay Jeddah, a very nice city overlooking the Red Sea. This strip along the Red Sea is known as the Hejaz. The Hejaz ancient trade route continues north toward Jordan and the Sinai Peninsula. This trade route would increase in importance for my understanding of Islam, but at this point I turned to the east and back into the Nejd.

All of these travels are better illuminated when the climate of the Nejd is factored in. Unlike many deserts, including some in North America, the Nejd doesn't appreciably cool at night. There are none of the "burn up during the day, freeze at night" complaints. In the eastern Sahara, where I spent some time in "field conditions" (living in a tent), it did cool off even on summer nights, and some dew could be noticed early in the morning. Not so in the Nejd. Try this: check the world's temperature highs and lows in your newspaper or on the 'Net. You will quickly see that Riyadh and Mecca are consistently among the hottest places on earth, often even during the northern hemisphere winter (southern hemisphere summer).

The Nejd becomes somewhat tolerable during the *Khamsin* (the "Fifty"). That is the approximate period in the Gregorian calendar winter during which some rain might be seen. This can result in rather surreal phenomena: consider what happens when the prevailing wind and rain from the west meets a wind-stirred sandstorm. It rains mud. I suppose you'd have to see it to believe it.

Another phenomenon is the humidity or lack thereof. The first Air Force briefing on most mornings was usually by the weather officer. Invariably, the senior officer asks about the humidity. In the Nejd, it is not uncommon to hear that it is 2 percent or less. The meteorological community used a "wet bulb" measurement that does not read humidity lower than 2 percent. In other words, it is as dry as dry can be. This causes an interesting leadership issue. It is so dry that perspiration is not evident, resulting in dehydration when you are not conscious that you're sweating. Thus, highly trained and motivated ground staff, especially maintenance people, want very much to finish their assigned work early. When it is less than 2 percent humidity with a temperature on the tarmac reaching 140 degrees, troops have to be ordered to spend basically half their time on break chugging bottled water. Some professional complaining ensues, but they all are able to come to work the next day.

How does this climate work? The Nejd runs the length of the Arabian Peninsula, from Jordan to the Rub al-Khali. In comparison with latitudes in the United States, it would lie to the south at about the same latitude as McAllen, Texas. To the north, it would be approximately the latitude of Oklahoma City. While those American cities enjoy temperate climates, they do tend to turn hot in the summer...but not 120 degrees day in and day out. The Nejd does not enjoy the common results of the jet stream, the Red Sea is not the Pacific Ocean (and across, it is largely more desert if you put any scientific store by it), and there is very little greenery and no snow. Simply put, cold fronts are definitely not attracted to the Nejd.

But there is a large group of people who are attracted by faith to traverse the Nejd. They are traveling to Mecca.

Flag of Saudi Arabia

The Saudi flag contains a central tenet of Islam:
"There is no God but Allah, and Mohammed is his prophet"

# 3

# Islam

" Submission to the will of Allah." That is the meaning of *Islam*. A *Moslem* is "one who submits." The Hejaz may host the holy cities of Mecca and Medina, but the Nejd is the intellectual heart of conservative Sunni Islam, adhering to the branch of Sunnism known as *Wahhabi* Islam.

Abdul Aziz ibn Saud did not seek to conquer the Nejd and the bulk of the Arabian Peninsula to gain access to oil or ports. He fought with his small but growing horse- and camel-mounted army to put in place the practice of Sunni Islam. To ibn Saud, this was worth the sacrifice and held a very special place for believing Arabs.

To understand the reason, we must start with the distinct differences between Sunni and Shi'a Islam. This is vital in understanding a long and often violent history. Very simply put, Sunnis believe that the best imam (or group of imams—a *ulema*, or religious council) should lead the faith. Observant Shi'as await the coming of "the next imam" in the lineage of the prophet Mohammed.[4] In about 680 AD, the two sects came into conflict, and this was when the time and place of battles were more or less chosen by the combatants. Thus, the Sunni army showed up in force, and battle was joined at Karbala, in present Iraq. The Shi'as ran late that day and were routed, includ-

---

4 Following the proper use of the title "prophet Mohammed," the blessing "May peace be upon him" is included for observant Moslems. The intent is that in all invocations of the prophet, this is silently implied.

ing the death of the only living male in the prophet's line, Hussain ibn Ali.

From what is known from a military perspective, the Shi'as were on a prideful fool's errand—thousands of Sunnis against less than a hundred Shi'as. Even given a better order-of-battle situation, the semiarid desert denied both sides a high-leverage maneuver position. To paraphrase Napoleon, Allah favored the side with the heaviest battalions. Nevertheless, Shi'as await the coming of the next imam. On the ninth and tenth of Moharram, the first month of the Islamic year, you will see young, devout young Shi'a men marching and flagellating themselves and chanting, "We'll be there next time, Hussain." Regarding the import of long memories, put it this way: given the same timeline, the Islamic residents of Jerusalem would still be out looking for the Knights of Malta. (As an aside of interest, during the Iran-Iraq War, the Iranians (who are Shi'as) named some of their offensives "Karbala."

Sunni Islam remains omnipresent in the Nejd. Again, it was through the Nejd that the founder of Saudi Arabia marched to roust the Al Rasheed dynasty. He was for his day a big man, and he engendered fierce loyalty. The present-day Nejd is a living testament to the strict Wahhabi branch of Islam practiced by ibn Saud. Wahhabi Sunnis believe in a literal interpretation of the Koran and the tenets of the Sharia, the corpus of law derived from the prophet Mohammed's teachings and writing. Islam may be practiced around the world as the fastest-growing faith in the world to a greater or lesser degree (Indonesia is the largest Islamic country). No such ambiguity in the Nejd.

There are some fundamentals to understanding Sunni Islam. Like other Islamic faiths, it has its "five pillars of Islam":

- The profession of faith. "There is no God but Allah, and Mohammed is his prophet." (This is written in Arabic above the scimitar on the Saudi flag.)
- Observance of the holy month of Ramadan. During the ninth month of the Islamic calendar, faithful Moslems fast from

daybreak to sunset (this rule is delayed for certain Moslems, such as RSAF aircrews). At the end of the month, a feast known as Eid al-Fitr is held. Ramadan is a bit like Christian Lent, but with much more denial of food and drink to reinforce humility and the sacrifice of faith.

- Pray facing Mecca five times a day.
- The giving of alms to the poor.
- If one is financially and physically able, undertake the hajj, the long pilgrimage to Mecca to symbolically reenact lessons from the Koran. To believers this is the most important pillar, and any Moslem who perishes making the Hajj is guaranteed passage to Allah. Prior to modern transportation, this was not uncommon in the Nejd.

These are specified in the Koran for Moslems. Practically, the hajj poses an oh-so-privileged burden on Saudi security and transportation infrastructure. There is good reason to emphasize its pervasive pace of life in the Nejd. It is almost as if the irresistible force of Westernization meets the unbreakable wall of the prophet's believers. The wall almost always wins.

Practitioners of the other monotheistic faiths may not be surprised that before Mohammed, idol worship and tribalism resulted in hundreds of statues of deities representing the various gods once worshipped in Arabia. The Koran surah (a brief chapter analogous to a chapter in the Christian Bible) 112:1–4 reads, "He is Allah, the One; the Eternal, the Absolute; He neither begets nor is born; there is none like Him." This is one of the fundamental doctrines of Islam. This is *tawheed* (Allah as one God), and *risalat* (prophets who came to guide humanity—of which the most prominent for Westerners is Jesus Christ) and *akhirah* (accountability in the hereafter). Additional attributes of Allah are in the Koran at surah 59:22–24. Islamic scholars point out that in Arabic, there is no plural of Allah, which reinforces the one-God doctrine. They may also opine that "Allah" is gender neutral (bear in mind that most languages assign gender to nouns, and some others have a neutral form), so whether Allah is a he or a she is never at issue. In English, however, it is "may *he* be praised."[5]

If you grant that Abraham was the father of Judaism through his son Isaac to King David and Solomon, that lineage leads by extension to Christ. The virgin birth, death, and resurrection are of course the nascency of Christianity, and Moslems recognize Christ as a major prophet. But for Moslems, the next step from Abraham is not to Isaac but to his half-brother Ishmael, who was cast into the desert with his mother Hagar, the bondwoman-turned-surrogate when Abraham's wife Sarah thought she was too old to conceive. Ishmael is perceived in some Islamic views as more significant than Isaac.

As noted earlier, Islam is the fastest-growing faith in the world, but at its core it is easier to understand with respect to the time and place of the prophet's revelations. He was cast out of Mecca around 622 AD and took refuge in Medina. He delivered the Koran as the word of Allah, conquering the multitheistic sects. If parts of the Koran seem familiar, it is with good reason. The prophet was from Mecca, a city astride the major trade route between current Yemen and the Holy Land. He would have been exposed to a variety of Jewish and Christian views and people, and Mecca even then was a significant city. The importance of the prophet to Moslems is due to his conveyance of the Koran after receiving it from Allah. He was clearly cognizant of other faiths, though, I argue, he lent to Islam a distinctly Arab interpretation.

It is also important to note that there is no warrant of divinity in Islam. Unlike in Christianity, the Prophet Mohammed is the *messenger* of Allah, not a godhead on earth or Allah's "son." The prophet did not align the Koran according to chronology, and it contains many stories that include other stories. The serious Moslem (or inquisitive infidel) may flip back and forth in the Koran. For Western infidels:

---

5 With recognition due to Imam Syed Hasan, PhD, of the Midland Islamic Council and more fully explored in "Voices of Faith," *Kansas City Star*, January 7, 2012.

I have found it useful to think of the Koran as one story over time (flip, flip) or multiple stories at one time.

Justice in the Nejd, it follows, is Koranic via the Sharia. Many in the West are somewhat justified in expressing contrary views of Sunni Islamic jurisprudence. Yes, it can involve beheading or stoning to death or loss of a hand. I am no apologist for such sentences, but I do note a substantial difference between what happened in *Death of a Princess* (a BBC work that I believe is somewhat dated), a case of a woman's stoning for adultery and the actual rules of Sharia evidence.

First, contrary to urban myth among Westerners in Riyadh, Arabs do not push Westerners to the front of Friday post-prayer crowds to force them to get a view of Islamic justice. They will clear a path for an infidel (even one with blue eyes), but I was never forced to the front.

[Note: what follows here is somewhat graphic—
if you prefer not to read it, please turn to the next page.]

The punishment for murder is a quick, all-business event. If an execution is scheduled, a black flag flies over Riyadh's Justice Square. The crowd flows from Riyadh's Grand Mosque (men come from inside it) to Justice Square ("Chop-Chop Square") after Friday's noon prayers. Room is made for an ambulance to drive into the plaza. The doomed convict is led from the ambulance, head covered. He is made to kneel, head down, above a basket. With what appears to be a large scimitar, the executioner takes one blow. The head drops into the basket, blood shooting from the headless body in a couple of strong squirts at first, and then to almost nothing as the blood pressure dissipates. The body and head are covered rapidly and placed quickly into the ambulance, which drives out of the plaza.

Other punishments include stoning a female adulteress to death (males in her family cast the first stone) and the loss of the right hand for robbery. The loss of the right hand carries a powerful stigma.

In the open desert, the left hand takes the place of toilet paper and therefore is not used in greeting or brought up to the level of where food is placed.

The rules of evidence are a bit difficult to decipher. My own understanding is largely through anecdotes of Arab friends. For murder and adultery, I was told that three or four Moslems (or two Moslems and three infidels) must witness the act for it to be prosecutable. Murder is somewhat understandable, but adultery? You'd have to really work at exhibitionism. For robbery, I was told the sentence is only rendered after three convictions, and then the hand is surgically removed. (Despite these examples, there is some beneficence in the strict Islamic corpus of law. Usury is forbidden, so no interest is charged in all-Saudi finance. The riyal is pegged to the US dollar at $1.00 to 3.75 riyals, so from a purely monetary perspective, as goes the dollar, so goes the riyal. How far does the jurisdiction reach, given a body of law based on religious belief? This is a rare issue in jurisprudence. It is perhaps intellectually simple to declare that jurisdiction extends as far as the borders of a nation-state based on its codified law. If I live in Belgium or Saudi Arabia, that settles it—I am subject to the laws of Belgium or Saudi Arabia and negotiated status of forces agreements for American troops on foreign soil. But the law's basis in the Sharia seem to imply an almost global scope—jurisdiction over all believers, no matter where they are. Perhaps the correct answer lies in the tradition of common law: what happens in the country governed by the custodian of the two holy cities of Mecca and Medina follows strict jurisdictional boundaries. As a matter of practice, they end when one leaves that country or from afar take action somewhere else.

A classic example comes from the airlines. When an aircraft crosses out of Saudi airspace, that fact is announced. This usually prompts women into a short queue for the restroom. They enter wearing the abaya and come out in nice conservative Western dress (although with head covered). Another example occurs with regularity on early Wednesday evenings as Saudi men board small buses to travel the King Fahd Causeway to the small island nation-state of Bahrain. The first segment is from Ad Dammam, SA to the Saudi security checkpoint, where there is some grumbling about the lone American who has to delay the bus to show his papers. The bus then travels to the Bahraini checkpoint, where the Saudis must show their credentials along with louder grumbling. The American notes that Bahrain is a predominantly a Shi'a country and regarded by some Saudis as rife with moral turpitude. One can consume alcohol in Bahrain and be served in better restaurants by comely expatriate young ladies. On one such trip, I saw and heard (in my failing Arabic) that a grandfather and grandson sitting in front of me were bound to Bahrain so the lad could learn more about "the birds and the bees."[6]

Finally, there is the Sharia rule forbidding reproduction of human facial images—and, among the most conservative Sunnis, the photography of anything. This comes from the fact that in Islamic art, the prophet's face is never portrayed. There is no Islamic counterpoint to, for instance, the images of Jesus Christ in homes and churches. By now, it may come as no surprise that I ran afoul of the *mutawa* while attempting to photograph the historic Mesmak Fortress in Riyadh. In the United States, it would be as if Lexington and Concord were off-limits to cameras. There are photographs of the al Saud and the country's leadership, but those are officially posed and see more exposure.

The discussion of the role of strict Wahhabi Islam in the life and history of the Nejd would rightly occupy multiple graduate school classes, with students accumulating three credit hours per course and more questions than answers. It extends to every facet of Nejdi life, including, as we are about to see, communication and culture.

---

6 You may have noticed no mention of the "(insert number of) virgins" supposedly promised in the Koran. The reason is that mainstream imams in the West, and the various Arabs whom I asked about the topic, either dismissed it as an unseemly topic or said there were a number of contradictory views.

# 4

# The Arabs

So, the sand, wind and heat, and conservative Wahhabi Sunni Islam are omnipresent in the Nejd. One other leg completes the triad that is the Nejd. Without its consideration, the brutal climate and the epicenter of Sunnism would leave a highly avoidable four hundred thousand square miles that would sap—not inspire—the unique traits that make the Nejd remarkable.

That element, of course, is the Arab people who are born to it and live their lives there. Theirs is not the feeling that their surroundings are per se undesirable. Remember the lone Bedou "breathing the desert"—theirs is a proud lot, bound by almost-iron ties of patrimony and familial and tribal loyalty along with an almost elitist view and a strong Bedouin influence. This attitude is not entirely explained by oil wealth or survival in a hostile region. It certainly is reinforced by the fact that the king (Abdullah), along with his "Sudairi Seven"[7] brothers in the past, is the guardian of the two holy cities of Mecca and Medina.

The Bedouin tradition is in strong evidence. The Bedouin still travel the Nejd as a way of life. At the outset of the First Gulf War, the Saudis opened a large desert grouping of basically multi-room, high-ceilinged condominiums as billeting for incoming foreign troops (primarily Americans). The buildings were unlived in and

---

7 Their mother's name was Sudairi.

even the interiors were covered with inches of desert sand. The name of the place is "Eskan Village." This is redundant since *eskan* means "village" in Arabic. It turns out that the entire sprawling complex had been built for the Bedouin, complete with camel-hitching rails (think of an old Western and the saloon with horses tied). The Bedouin, I was told, did not want to live in one place and did not occupy the Village.

The Bedouin influence is found even in sport and socializing. Camels are raced, falconry is favored over golf,[8] dune buggies roam over the desert, and entertainment is offered in a very traditional way. Invited to a prominent Saudi's desert compound, you'd find at least one large tent with rugs and pillows throughout. Lamb, mutton, or beef is grilled, and the leader or host engages guests in a relaxed setting with wonderful tea. A fancier meal is a mini-fortress of rice around a pool of lamb or goat meat. Using the right hand only, guests take a handful of rice soaked with the meat broth and some vegetables and pop it in. (While seated on the ornate carpet, take care not to show the soles of the feet toward an Arab—it is a significant insult.)

Another traditional Bedouin celebration is the *arhda*, a dance during which Saudi males holding swords go through intricate steps, at the appointed time thrusting the blade upward, including one of the most famous of photographs of the country's leadership.

The long and the short of it is that we have here the continuance of the same traditions practiced for millennia and practiced by Abdul Aziz ibn Saud when he consolidated modern Saudi Arabia. From the Nejd he came and in the Nejd he conquered. The Nejdi

---

8 Golf is played, however. You carry your tee with you and every shot is an approach shot to the "green"—an oiled flat of sand. Once you are on the "green" (or "brown")—since the oiled sand holds golf balls really well—there is a piece of PVC pipe about 4" diameter, cut lengthwise and placed at the ball and the cup. And you putt away. One-putts are, to no one's great surprise, common.

desert is quite understandably a source of pride for the Arabs living there.

There is also an incredibly strong sense of patriarchal and familial bonding. If jurisprudence is exercised regarding women in ways we may see as extreme, the practices are not without Bedouin influence and are based in how they view families. The males are the heads of families, expected to take wives that become a part of the groom's family. With females barred from driving (a topic being reexamined there as of this writing) or even riding in the front seat, mandatory wear of the abaya, no voting rights (such as they are in the kingdom), for the Westerner, for all intents and purposes, women are treated as second-class citizens.

A Saudi male coworker (an RSAF fighter pilot trained in the United States) had a different explanation predicated on the survival instinct of the Bedouin. He said that to the Nejd Arabs, the logical approach was to tie family honor to the virtue and treatment of women. He pointed out the numerous stores selling beautiful dresses and lingerie, arguing that while it seemed to the Western eye that women were stifled, in reality they were treated like queens in their homes. Among the Bedouin since time immemorial, the virtue and childbearing responsibilities of women were treasured, and Allah be praised that the prophet recognized this. That was the reason the Sharia dealt so harshly with "wayward women." In other cultures, my Saudi source said it was his belief that Western women tried to look their best when going out into the world, either socially or professionally, but were denied that appreciation at home.

This last view is an example of a subtle elitism: that "real" Arabs enjoy life in ways that others don't. It is hard to argue against that in context—maybe Arabs do have the luxury to look down on infidels to some degree, and even perhaps on expatriate Moslems. Anyone who has spent time in the conservative Nejd can sense a fairly definite pecking order. First come adherent Arab (or "Saudi")

Moslems. Second, the developed-world Moslems, followed by other-world Moslems. Sliding in next as well regarded are educated Westerners—even better if they are military officers or non-commissioned officers (NCOs). (It is interesting that within the second number, one of the most popular American Moslems is… Muhammad Ali. While I was living in the Nejd, the boxing legend made an *umrah*, a pilgrimage to Mecca outside of the hajj period. He is a darling of the Arab press.) At the bottom rung is the developing-world infidel—the "Gastarbeiter" from places such as the Philippines, Sri Lanka, and so on, who work as laborers sending money back to their home countries (more to follow). As we say down on the farm, "ain't gonna happen in Araby."

Of course, there are no bars, there is only one favorite team, and the mixing of men and women won't fly (though even recognizing the existence of same-sex couples would never happen). But it's more than that. Given the strong ties to family and tribe, "guarded but cordial" is an understated way to estimate the Arab approach to new people. It is not meant to offend you, but it takes more than a cursory introduction—or even daily contact over time—before one can call an Arab a "friend," and that will take place at the time and place of his or her choosing. This is not standoffishness, but rather the way relations are conducted in the Nejd. Two other issues are not in debate. First, if you make an Arab friend, the friendship will be taken seriously. Second, expect an Arab to lighten up on a visit to you in the United States, Europe, or elsewhere.

Art in brass based on the Koran

# 5

# Arabic, Art, and the Astral Plain

ere's a think piece to consider. You speak the prominent language of your native country—its lingua franca, if you will. Now compare the language and appreciation of it among native speakers as a ratio. For instance, let's surmise the benchmark is American English. How many Americans appreciate it? Granted, Americans have created some great literature, but English is primarily used for immediate communication. Though "http:" and ".com" mean something to English speakers, I assert that the ratio of English speakers to appreciators of the mother tongue is 1:1.

Now let's go to the United Kingdom. English is still the mother tongue there, and even today, writers such as Blake, Coleridge, and the Bard of Avon are as popular as ever. Correct English usage is a mark of higher class (and then there is the perception in America that somehow, a British accent means the speaker is smarter). In light of this, let's give the UK a 3:1—Brits treasure English more than Americans do.

Now to the Nejd. Arabic is much, much more than a means of communication there. The language of Islam and the Koran, Arabic is used to create art symbolically, either inscribed with elaborate calligraphy or as an objet d'art that usually echoes the shape of something in the natural world.

And, even though Arabs can be a bit standoffish in a social or personal context, the visitor can easily break the ice by asking to learn basic Arabic phrases. In the waning days of the Iran-Iraq War, the RSAF took possession of American-built E-3A airborne warning and control system (AWACS) aircraft and KC-135 air refueling tankers. Having been assigned aircrew duties onboard the US AWACS, I was assigned to fly on the new Saudi aircraft as well. The patrols were long—up to twelve hours or more—and I did not really have much to do at my console.

The Saudi airplanes had the requisite aft bunks, comfortable airline-style seats away from the consoles, an area for the prayer rug amidships (one of the navigator's tasks was to always know the aircraft's position relative to Mecca), and fantastic in-flight food. I would generally get up after a couple of hours looking at Gulf airspace and make my way forward to the Saudi aircrew. There, I would suggest my Arabic was not good and that I was studying to improve. In every case, a Saudi officer would spring up from his console and offer an extended tutoring session in "proper Arabic." He would usually bring paper and pen, choose a pair of the plusher seats, and delve with great animation into my airborne Arabic lesson. Often he would go so far as to tell the ranking mission crew commander that the American was trying to learn Arabic and that he would be away from his duty station for a while. The commander always nodded assent, and in English, within earshot of me, told the teacher that if the pupil needed more help to please let him know.

This attitude and enthusiasm were not limited to the men on long aircraft patrols. In the New Gold Souq, a shopkeeper who once surrendered a group of us to the *mutawa* would animatedly engage Americans who showed the slightest inclination to learn Arabic. He had an ace up his sleeve, too. Realizing that the bulk of the small number of deployed airmen were stationed at Tinker Air Force Base near Oklahoma City, he stuck an "Oklahoma is OK!" bumper sticker to a free space on the wall of his souq and never failed to use it to teach "hello" (*salaam alaykum*), "good-bye, peace" (*mysalaama*), "yes" (*na'am*), and "no" (*laa*).

Another case comes from the framed brass Arabic example at the top of this chapter. I purchased it in what might be called an Islamic bookstore. You learn to haggle in the Nejd, as in many other places. In the Arab world, not to tender a counter-offer to have the merchant defend his precious holdings is almost an insult to him. And, very clearly an infidel, I haggled over this beautiful rendering of a surah from the Koran. We went back and forth, and I finally talked him into its sale. I was grinning like a Cheshire cat as I carefully boarded the bus and mailed my item to myself in the United States as quickly as I could get to the American post office. Since I walked frequently past the shop, I wanted it to be unavailable if he decided he wanted it back.

Then there is the topic of Arabic translation into English (and many other languages). You may have noticed that I've employed "Mohammed," "Moslem," and other Arabic words that could just as well be read in English as "Muhammed" or "Muslim." The question of how we spell these terms is just the tip of the iceberg. Consider how many spellings of "Qaddafi" were seen when that tyrant was about, or, for that matter, spellings of "Hussain." Geographic place names are in the same position. "Al Iskandaria" is Alexandria, Egypt, and "Ar Riyadh" is the district in which the Saudi capital is located. Please pardon this phenomenon, remembering that Arabic is known in the West as a "super hard" language, almost as challenging to Western language native speakers as English—the world's most difficult language to learn—is to the Arabs.

Arabic is a Semitic language with origins in the ancient language of Aramaic. It surprises some to learn that it is a linguistic cousin of modern Hebrew, a reminder that the Arab-Israeli conflict is about land considered holy, not every aspect of the two societies (you'll understand that this conflict is a little too complex for the present work). Some will chortle at the notion that I'd like to study Aramaic, and they likely have insight I do not possess. But just as Latin is the source of many Indo-European languages, Aramaic is the foundation of Semitic languages like Arabic and Hebrew.

Let's return to the ratio of language speakers and language appreciators. My conservative estimate for Arabic is 10:1:1—Arabic is *art* for the Arabs. Which brings up another question—what else is art for the Arabs? Arab art tends along the same lines as art throughout the Islamic and Arabic- or Farsi-speaking world. Given that the portrayal of the human face has no prominence (and in some quarters is deemed irreverent), art has taken a different turn. I am no art critic, but it doesn't take a rocket scientist to see three major themes predominate. These are Islam, the natural world, and repetitive patterns. Islam we have touched upon, and nothing called "art" can go far wrong by combining Islam and Arabic.

The natural-world-based art is interesting, since its "subject matter" tends to come from the desert (the Nejd specifically), but it portrays a vast array of plants and animals nowhere to be seen on real local landscapes. I contend that this makes sense: Allah's heaven has the elements the real world lacks, including lots of water and greenery. There is a reason the Saudi flag is white on a green background. And for decades, the Libyan flag was just a plain, green field. Thus, while there is an impressive corpus of Islamic art directly, Islam also influences the portrayal of the natural world, with topics such as winding grape vines and animals not found in Arabia. This school of design that can be found on floors and in wall hangings throughout the globe. The "Persian" carpet contains designs from not only Iran but the desert Middle East too. The inspired Arab art of repetitive motifs is familiar around the world. Be it the repetition of a natural theme, such as trees or leaves, or the more abstract use of embellished squares, circles, or other basic geometric forms.

In the Nejd and elsewhere, we find Islamic "prayer rugs," the topic of which is usually the Grand Mosque in Mecca or a repetitive motif. These are smaller rugs designed to be carried around for use at prayer time (the Saudis even had one placed amidships on their AWACs aircraft). The prayer rugs are smaller and less expensive, but in their finest form they are legitimate works of art. During the Soviet occupation of Afghanistan, specifically "war" rugs, replete with images of AK-47s, Soviet fighting vehicles, and helicopters, were woven as both political statements and sources of funding for the then-Mujahedeen (although there is no evidence they ever competed with opium poppies in Afghanistan). The markets around Peshawar and other border Pakistani towns included this carpet type as a tenuous and hidden aspect of that war, and some of them made their way to the Arabian Peninsula. I always thought that the single or crossed scimitar of the Saudi flag and crest were a more telling statement on the history they are designed to represent.

A side benefit of spending time in the rug souqs with experienced Arabists were their lessons in estimating the value of a rug. Basically, any rug you might consider purchasing should be folded back to reveal the underside. You are looking for stitching all the way through. Check the end tassels to ensure they are integral to the rug. Keep an eye on the shopkeeper. If you act like you know what you are doing and he winces (in my case, it had to be Academy Award-quality acting), you know it probably is an overpriced, inferior product. If he comes over to show off his rug, prepare to haggle if you really want it.[9] Having said that, if you befriend an Arab, follow his or her advice and take mental notes. They will behave as if born to haggle. That is because they *were* born to haggle.

If your haggling is cut short by the call to prayer and you are in the Nejd, you can be assured that Moslems in the Eastern Province are already at prayer, and those in the Hejaz will be in a few minutes. That is because the time-space continuum is extremely important in everyday Nejdi life.

---

9 This technique works all over. In Egypt, for example, if you take a corner of a piece of papyrus and crumple it, if you see a wince, you know it is not real. Genuine papyrus is almost impossible to tear.

The Islamic world works on Islamic time. The calendar is based on lunar phases, not on solar effects as with the modern Gregorian calendar. This means an Islamic month is 28.5 days, so in the space of three and half decades, the calendars will overlap and the cycle continues. This is important for a number of reasons, not the least of which is that climate behaves according to solar cycles. Those concerned with hajjis arriving, the sandstorms of the *Khamsin*, and other major events must plan on significant differences from decade to decade. That's OK, because the Arabs have a word to deal with uncertainty or indecision: *"enshallah"*—"as Allah wills." This can become frustrating to Westerners: "The nine o'clock meeting will begin by nine thirty, enshallah." There is always time for another small cup of real Arab tea, the tea leaves steeped with mint, and a breakfast of unleavened bread, sprinkled with spices.

I was accustomed to a particular ritual almost every morning, sitting with my Arab counterparts as they spoke English and helped me with Arabic. Several key lessons I learned revolved around "enshallah." First, after your third cup of tea, unless you really, really want more (which you will), you waggle the small teacup unobtrusively from side to side, and it will be picked up. Second (and I embarrassingly knew much better), do not outwardly show or speak admiration of something you see belonging to an Arab, because the code of the Bedouin then demands the host make a gift of that item to you. I made this mistake when I mentioned the tea we were having one morning was excellent and that I wished I knew how to make it for when I returned to the States. The next morning, waiting for me were two large bundles of tea leaves and mint, a silver teapot, and instructions in English for proper preparation.

As an aside, the number three carries a great deal of meaning in the Nejd, which I attribute to both Wahhabi Islam and the tradition of the Bedouin. A stranger coming into a Bedouin camp is welcomed to the same food and the very limited creature comforts as one's own family or tribe—that is true for three nights. Then it is time for the visitor to leave. There also tend to be three days of travel from oasis to oasis, and while the humans may grow thirsty the camels will, too, eventually. The import of "three" is deeply rooted in the intense introspection of Arab faith, along with other traditions. The "blood debt," for instance, calls not for ad hominem justice but for a sacrifice from the offender's family or tribe. In the Western world, a murderer is personally sentenced to pay for the crime against person and society. In the Arab world, if someone from another tribe kills one of yours, your retribution in kind can be aimed at anyone with whom the killer is closely associated (criminal, victim, and criminal's family).

But back to the time-space continuum. One of the fascinating events of the Islamic year is the identification of the full moon as it heralds the holy month of Ramadan, the ninth month of the Islamic year. In another Bedouin tradition, men go to the easternmost place on the Arabian Peninsula. Upon confirmation (enshallah) of the moon, haste is made by either camel or cell phone to inform the king in his capacity as the custodian of the two holy cities of Mecca and Medina. Those who identified the moon are then sent to the king and received in his *majlis*. (The *majlis* is a surprise to those new to the Nejd. At it, any male Moslem may directly petition the monarch for relief, remedy, or favor, and they are welcome so to do.) The spotting of the Ramadan moon is of particular significance. As with much in the Nejd, it can be new to Westerners, who on occasion operate on a different agenda, namely that the Western mind will have already calculated the moon phase.

# 6

## Not-So-Innocents Abroad

I have mentioned the expatriates living and working in the Nejd. Some who were there in the late 1980s probably ought not to read this chapter. They can just be happy that this is not a kiss-and-tell book and that no names will be used (except in accolades, perhaps). Neither will I address the hundreds of thousands of US and allied troops who deployed in support of Operations Desert Storm and Iraqi Freedom. All were certainly notable, but we'll stick to that period when, in the Nejd, the Western "footprint" was growing smaller, bit by bit.

This chapter could easily carry the subtitle "No One Is in the Nejd without a Story." Between the US military, nurses working in the several large hospitals, other civilians—ranging from Harvard lawyers working for princes to the men who worked in the airport control towers to some of the coaches of Saudi national sports teams—everyone was there for a reason. For the military, it was an assignment. For the others, there were a variety of reasons. Money topped the list, but you also learned that some went to the most non-Western place they could find so they could leave something else behind. The cohort was rather like a well-paid, English-speaking, co-ed Foreign Legion.

In any case, it made for the chance to meet a lot of very interesting people. The upscale place to be on Riyadh Wednesday nights—the equivalent of the American Friday start of the weekend—was the Camel's Breath Saloon. The Saloon was named appropriately after the Hog's Breath Saloon in Fort Walton Beach, Florida, a panhandle spring break hotspot located within a stone's throw of two air force bases. The Camel's Breath was on the grounds of the US Military Training Mission, walled and gated off from Saudi society. Military and civilian men who drove came up solo and stopped near a queue of abaya-clad women before entering the grounds. The car stopped, and three females climbed into the back seat. The male driver, who could bring three guests into the Mission, pulled in to park near the Camel's Breath. It should be no surprise that the young ladies were out of their abayas by the time the car was turned off.

And in we went to the Camel's Breath. It had very close seating, a dance floor, and a large—you guessed it—bar. On my first visit, I was greeted by a somewhat tipsy Aussie who yelled his name above the music and a "New, are you, mate? Grab yourself a beer and go talk to a sheila! G'day, mate." He was the Australian coach of the Saudi national tennis team. The place was packed. I picked out a couple of AWACs officers I knew, but we could have been in the bar scene in the first *Star Wars*, just with better-looking characters. In the course of a few Wednesday evenings, I was befriended by Neal, one of the aforementioned Harvard lawyers, and John, an air traffic controller at Riyadh Air Base. I also started going out with a British nurse ("out" meant going to someone's apartment until I was granted a place in a walled compound).

Those evenings, to this day, constituted the best parties I have ever attended. It was as if everyone had worked in the Saudi system all week and now could cut loose. There was no pretense and no apparent egos. The prettiest woman in the place would say yes if the worst-looking guy asked her to dance. And when you combined the senses of humor of the Americans, Brits, Canadians, and Aussies, it was an absolute riot. At first, I wondered where the libations in the well-stocked bar came from—there was never any shortage. (The only thing the "gentlemen" drivers had to worry about was the Saudi equivalent of a DUI, but no one knew of any Westerner getting one.)

The question of where the libations came from was answered in the fullness of time: the American expatriates, at least, who were there on permanent-party status each received a "tea ration." As I recall, one American could order ten cases of beer, a case of wine, or several fifths of something stronger. I never knew what the other country nationals received, but all of it taken together made up considerably more drink than you would have expected in the middle of the Nejd.

I kept in touch with Neal and John while I was there (Neal would end up hosting dinner for me and two other airmen during Operation Desert Shield—an entirely different story—but Neal made sure some comely, intelligent young ladies were also in attendance). He scored big by being retained by a Saudi prince. John made it big by watching and acting on a great idea. He spent his time as the only controller present at Riyadh AB, and I went to visit him. It appalled me that an active base had one controller on duty (good aircraft landing stories abounded). While he was up there, he realized that a runway had to be closed for days, if not weeks, for cleaning, which mostly involved removing rubber from superheated tires touching down. The rubber, if left untouched, formed a slick at both departure and arrival ends of the runways.

On one of his mandatory "environmental morale leave" (EML) periods, he returned to his home state of North Carolina and went snooping around its Research Triangle area. He secured marketing and distribution sales and licensing rights for a quick method to clean runways for not just Saudi Arabia, but several other hot-weather Middle Eastern countries. He basically offered the ability to clean the runway with a pavement Zamboni, taking not days or weeks, but a single day per runway. ("If I were a rich man...")

John had also perfected a technique to make homebrewed hard liquor. I'd swing past his compound on the way back from the air base, and he would have bottles of the ferocious stuff. I was cautious. The similar "sadiq" liquor, I was told, could cause blindness due to a lack of quality control. John was fine with it.

I've referred to walled compounds a couple of times. They are ubiquitous in developed areas of the Nejd (driving past desert, more desert, a camel pen, more desert, walled compound, more desert...). The Saudis put up certain expatriates in them, and I went to an all-American compound just west of downtown Riyadh. Remember that "tea ration"? You'd pick up your ration, save what you wanted, and donate the rest to the common cooler—which was located under an awning next to a perfect pool. It was de rigueur to go into the compound, change into shorts, and head for the pool, where the party was generally underway. In keeping with Saudi sensitivities, the compound was segregated by gender. Wait, change that—the compound was *supposed* to be segregated.

So, suffice it to say that while some of us spent more time poking around the desert, the Americans and those from the British Commonwealth found that all was not drudgery and money. The same could not be said for the manual laborers from the developing world. In Arab eyes, blued-eyed American officers with facial hair (which is expected of Saudi men when they can grow it) were below Arabs, but not too far. The manual laborers were quite another story. They had come from their world to work for a pittance on the Arabian Peninsula, but that pittance was vastly more than they could earn in the Philippines or Sri Lanka or wherever they came from. Their meager clothing was as dirty as an oil worker's, but the laborers were not making their gold in the "liquid gold" sector.

# 7

What do you think of when the Arabian Peninsula or Saudi Arabia is mentioned? You would be in the clear majority if your answer was "oil." It is a populist vision spurred on by media reportage featuring an oil expert or politician stating that "we must reduce our dependence on Middle Eastern oil." Capacious histories and analysis are best found elsewhere (to wit, Daniel Yergin's *The Prize*), but I would be remiss in not touching on this most pervasive of topics. "Oil" conjures images of the 1972–1973 oil crisis, the 1979–1980 Iranian oil crisis, and most recently, the "blood for oil" sloganeering aimed at US military involvement in Southwest Asia (and, as of this writing, potential Iranian action). Let us back away for a moment and clarify a few points.

First, the United States is *not* dependent on any particular producing nation or, as in the early 1970s, a cartel within a cartel (the Organization of Arab Petroleum Exporting [OAPEC] being part of the Organization of the Petroleum Exporting Countries [OPEC]). The 1970s oil crisis was indeed one of the very few successful results of applying an economic weapon.[10] The permanent (and considerable) price increase after these crises fundamentally altered the framework of oil prices. In the case of OAPEC, the Arab-Israeli conflict added a great deal of tinder to the economic fire. More on oil pricing later.

---

10 See Gary Hufbauer, et. al., *Economic Sanctions Reconsidered* for detailed analysis of economic embargoes and sanctions.

Second, the United States and the rest of the world are dependent on global oil *markets*. Trading floors around the world would be less entertaining to watch if the stakes were not so high. Neither the Saudis nor any other single country controls the price of oil, although the Saudis have long played a "swing producer" role when it is in their interest. Saudi Arabia remains a single-resource economy, and it is not in its interest to have the world scurrying for alternative fuels when it is economically beneficial for consumer nations. The Saudis have never had a net loss in proven oil and natural gas (combined, they are petroleum) reserves. While other producer states feel the need to maximize short-term profits, the Saudis would prefer long-term demand.

For years, the Saudis used their swing producer role to moderate prices, again to sustain demand. As of this writing, recent Saudi decisions to lift their production ceiling to accommodate globally higher prices at above $100 per barrel were welcomed by other producing nations. Previously, the Saudis had aimed at about $85 per barrel. The Saudis quietly telegraphed this by increasing their surcharge on oil bound for China and India and by increasing their production, and then accepting prices above $100 per barrel in early 2012.

This makes a fair amount of economic sense as far as a cost-benefit analysis. Don't the Saudis want to keep countries like the United States from finding energy options? Yes, they do, but that appears to be outweighed by another factor: Chinese and Indian demand is soaring. (Though the Chinese economy is raging upward, I believe it is a huge bubble.) The Saudis want to ensure those two markets are dependent more than they want to discourage US and European development of alternative energy. My take is that the Saudis also realize the tenuous future of the Chinese economy and would like nothing better than firm Chinese dependence on Gulf oil. Yes, if (when) the Chinese bubble bursts, Chinese demand will probably not decrease. But if it does, Gulf oil producers will have secured a beachhead that cannot be shaken. This makes a fair amount of economic sense as far as a cost-benefit analysis.

But as far as the Nejd, this is putting the cart before the camel. The Nejd matters because it is anchored by the capital, and therefore, key Saudi oil decisions are taken there. But the oil itself is concentrated in the Eastern Province, convenient to Arabian Gulf shipping and still protected by both US and Saudi military power. On the west lie Mecca and Medina in the Hejaz, the holiest cities in Islam. Abdul Aziz ibn Saud came across the area we now call Kuwait, directly into the Nejd. He crossed that barren expanse to defeat the competing tribal forces and came to control the entire area now known as Saudi Arabia (try to find another country named for a family). You've read it already, but it bears repeating: oil was not in the sights of Abdul Aziz in the early 1920s. He was, first and foremost, acting to secure the Nejd for Wahhabi Sunni Islam, and he found important allies in the Bedouin of the Nejd. His key victory was at the Mesmak Fortress in Riyadh. Mecca and Medina he undoubtedly wanted to control. The oil probably was the largest bonus in history, but the record indicates he appreciated the largess it granted. However, in his lifetime, he clearly did not count on the massive returns his progeny would receive. Those sons have been kings ever since. As you've read, they are known as the Sudairi Seven, all boys of Abdul Aziz with his wife named Sudairi. The current king is Abdullah, preceded by Fahd, Khalid, and Faisal. King Faisal, architect of the 1970s embargo, was lambasted in the West at the time but in the light of history appears as a steady hand guiding the kingdom with due consideration, given the Arab-Israeli conflict.

The story is widely told—though I have not seen it completely documented—that when oil revenues started to pay off, Abdul Aziz kept the kingdom's treasury in a locked trunk in his bedchamber. That would be in keeping with his lifelong priorities. The Saudis have adroitly used the kingdom's wealth to minimize the tumult of 2011's Arab Spring, although we could argue that it was less vulnerable to the dissatisfaction that boiled over first in Tunisia and then in short order in Libya and Egypt. (As of this writing, it rages still in Syria.) In other words, I don't believe that the motivations that spurred violence and autocratic leadership overthrows are present in Saudi Arabia, and they appear to be waning in Jordan. Oil has provided the Saudis a cushion in that regard, but as we shall see, it presents profound challenges as well.

The Arab Peninsula, showing the Sinai, Straits of Hormuz, and Bab El Mandeb

# 8

## Strategic Thoughts

"Strategic" and "strategic interests" mean the fundamental under-lying positions, advantages, and threats to a particular land-mass, ocean, or usually a region and either estimation or knowledge of the national and transnational players in that area (obviously there is a huge body of work on the topic). The Nejd has seen its share of the ramifications of great power politics and great power competition. It goes much deeper. For example, there was the process of neutralizing German-Turkish influence in the Hejaz and part of the Nejd during and after WWI,[11] which included the British striking a deal that upon the evacuation of the Sharif of Mecca, his two sons would effectively get their own countries. They became monarchs of Jordan and Iraq. Obviously, Iraq became dominated by overthrows and violence that has not yet ended. In Jordan, a Hashemite King still reigns; after years of enlightened leadership by King Hussain, his son Abdullah has ascended to the throne.

As I've said, I believe the House of Saud need not, in the long term, concern itself over the possibility of sharing the fate of autocrats in Tunis, Tripoli, and Cairo. The events there, however, merely scratch the surface of the strategic importance of the Arabian Peninsula. One consideration is that to the north and southwest, Riyadh has shaky governments with which to deal with in Iraq and Yemen. The

---

11 This is where "Lawrence of Arabia" gained his fame.

Saudis continue to keep a wary eye on Iran, which seems to require keener vision by the week. The US "Global War on Terrorism" is a conundrum for the Saudis; while there is little doubt in Foggy Bottom about continued US support for the kingdom, a majority of the 9/11 hijackers were Saudis. At the same time that very high levels in both governments agree on this point, the Saudis (many of whom in the upper strata of the royal family took their college education in the United States) are also aware of the American-on-the-street's view of their wealth and the stereotypes that attend it.

The latter point is a lesson not just in analysis of the Nejd but is applicable as academics, diplomats and world leaders are very aware: they know more about us than we collectively know about them. This engenders an understanding on their part that goes beyond the sale of Levi's and black-market Lady Gaga CDs and adverts featuring the Marlboro Man. Typically, Saudi princes have spent years in the West and are very attuned to the deeper elements affecting US power projection in Southwest Asia. I cannot counsel an adequate response—this is just the way it is—but we are well advised to at least be aware of their view of us.

We can indulge in a bit of old fashioned geopolitical analysis, no longer at the fore as we face nontrinitarian threats.[12] The three circles on the map above show three sea lines of communication (SLOC) chokepoints impacting not only the Arabian Peninsula but world maritime trade and force projection. At the Mediterranean entrance to the Red Sea is, of course, the Suez Canal. For about eleven years under Gamal Abdul Nasser, it was intentionally blocked. That forced the much longer sail around Africa. Now, of course, it is open. There is even an oil tanker known as a "Suez Max" for its hull designed to transit the Suez Canal. While no threat appears immi-

---

12 "Trinitarian" is Martin van Crevald's term referring to the way the interests of a state's people, its formal military, and its government were once theorized to operate as the state honored international norms of warfare. Obviously, al-Qaida, the Taliban, the IS, and the Houthi don't participate in this model (see van Crevald's *The Transformation of War*).

nent, since it was reopened, the canal appears as an assumed passage for trade- and warships alike.

The next chokepoint is the oft-mentioned Strait of Hormuz. (The Strait of Hormuz wins first prize in the "how-often-mentioned" category any day.) To the south lies a small, separate finger of Oman. To the north and along the entire length of the Strait sits a bellicose Iran. Little attention is paid to the oceanography of the strait's shipping lanes. For inbound and outbound ultra large crude carriers (ULCCs), there is a limited space along the Omani side of the Straits where these monsters can pass. The threat obviously is posed by Iran, who decades ago started to pay attention to the deployment of shore-to-surface anti-ship missiles.

The third chokepoint is an overlooked ocean constraint known as the Bab el-Mandab. If a ship is meant to sail from the Mediterranean to the Indian Ocean, it must go through the Bab el-Mandab and the Suez Canal. Given the increasingly dicey neighborhood in which it sits, this chokepoint deserves more attention. To its east sits the rather unstable state of Yemen. The collection of problems to its west are many—most recently, Somalia pirates taking both tankers and oceangoing pleasure craft. There is an immediate threat to the Bab el-Mandab, but that is overlooked (particularly in the West) due more to the noise level of the Iranian threats to Hormuz than it is to the value of the Bab el-Mandab.

All three of these nodes have the potential to dramatically affect Saudi Arabia and the Nejd (and, indeed, the world). Even if there is only transitory, temporary interruption of any of the three, at the very least we can count on the predictable irrationality of oil specifically and commodities markets in general. Not just oil is at play. You can bet that the Saudis see this. Recent developments near the Nejd are ample indication that both nature and regional power abhor a vacuum. It is a grand dichotomy that the region that gave rise to the apparent permanence of the three major monotheistic faiths is characterized by violent challenge and change. As of this writing, for the Arabian Peninsula this includes the rise of the Islamic State (IS or ISIS) in the vacuum of northwestern Iraq and eastern Syria, and the Iranian-backed Houthi Islamic threat in Yemen in the vacuum of that failed state.

Moderate Arab leaders can tolerate neither. Nearest the Nejd and overlooking the Bab El Mandeb, the latter will be dealt with first. Combined Arab forces have organized to neutralize the Houthi Shi'a extremist threat first, and I suspect by this reading will have installed a more legitimate government in Yemen. The existence of the threat to begin with shows the destabilizing role of Iran in the region, however. The Saudis cannot tolerate such a presence on their southern border.

Likewise with moderate Arab tolerance of the IS. One may ask why Sunni states would object to an extremist Sunni group. Simply, "conservative" and "extremist" mean two completely different things in the Arab world. The sheer brutality shown by the IS alone is reason for conservative Sunnis to counter them. Also overlooked is that the IS leader, al-Baghdadi, has insisted his followers pray to him as Caliph. That is not the way Sunnis select the leadership of the faith. Interestingly, Iran and Syria also have an interest in countering the IS. Rather a sort of "the enemy of my enemy is my friend" situation, but with very unholy bedfellows.

Both situations offer a bit of good news for the United States. We provide support to the Saudis and other Arab allies – weapons systems, intelligence, logistics, etc., to be sure. But after two long and costly wars in Iraq and Afghanistan, against the Houthis in Yemen and largely against the IS, our Arab allies are doing it themselves. Against the Shi'a Houthis, the Arabs have assembled an eight-country joint Arab effort led by Saudi Arabia. It is somewhat more complicated against the IS (American troops provide air and training support including Iraqi and Syrian forces), but does not involve large formations of American "boots on the ground."

Controversial writer Ayaan Hirsi Ali -controversial because she was raised a Moslem and now writes and speaks against Islam – her most recent book is <u>Heretic</u>, about the need for reformation in Islam (similar to the Reformation of the Christian church) said that of all violent casualties in the world, 70% were Moslem versus Moslem. Her numbers have come into question, but with Shi'a extremists in Yemen and Sunni extremists in Anbar Province, Iraq and points east, south and west, that would seem to be the case.

Returning to the complications in coordinating fighting the IS, some of the forces are national (such as the Iraqi military), others are fighting for anti-IS causes they espouse (ranging from Sunni and Shi'a tribal militias to the Kurds). These varying motivations have to be recognized by both moderate Arabs and the West. Second, even a brief glance at the IS videos shows training for rather recognizable insurgent, organized warfare. This rather standard approach puts the IS into a unit-organized form of fighting that puts their forces into alignments that require logistics, communications and open command-and-control. It also shows the sheer brutality, almost evil for evil's sake, the IS practices.

Compare this to Al-Queda and the Taliban. Both seek secrecy in hidden strongholds and both have criticized the IS approach. Despite this, one of the big winners in these hyper-violent scenarios is Al-Queda, and particularly AQ-AP (Al-Queda Arabian Peninsula) who has stealthy moved to take over key facilities, including an oil export port in Yemen. And Al Queda remains focused on their corrupted view of who they fight, without the "kill everyone not exactly like us" approach of the IS.

So for the Nejd, a major headache looms to the north, and its ankle is shackled. The response to the question "when will this end?" is unfortunately "not in our lifetimes." That depressingly means the violence around the Nejd. The Nejd itself is meant to last much longer, *enshallah*.

# 9

Epilogue

few final observations about the Nejd. The first is a foreboding but future fact. While today you would probably rank the overall needs of the world as energy (oil) first and food and water second, within a decade I predict they will be precisely reversed. Humans can go a long period without oil if need be - certainly at high economic and convenience cost - but survivable. Additionally, humans can go, we are told, three weeks without food. As for water, we can last three days. Clearly, water is a resource on an easily anticipated increase in demand.

When I left for European assignment, I considered this would be problematic for the Nejd. Saudi Arabia, along with other countries (most notably China) have long tapped underground aquifers, and they were being sucked dry. During WWII, President Franklin Delano Roosevelt met with Abdul Aziz on a US ship in the Red Sea. FDR asked aides how deep Saudi water was in the aquifer. Told it was fairly near the surface (within twenty feet or so), the president asked the Saudi leader why it was not used for agriculture. Abdul Aziz's response was that he was an old man and unable to consider agriculture. In any case, Saudi Arabia was running out of spring water.

That is no longer true. Saudi Arabia is now a global leader in the desalination of water, including the world's largest desalination facility at Ras Al Khair. Water desalination is an energy-intensive endeavor, particularly the favored reverse-osmosis process. Needless to say, that is not a problem for the Saudis, but they have also taken advantage of another natural asset – the sun – by powering a desalination facility using a massive solar farm. It is not beyond the pale that FDR's agriculture in the desert notion could be answered in the affirmative.

Second, (though it may in the midterm be number one), a crucial demand-supply dilemma was, surprisingly, oil. Or, more specifically, refined petroleum product—such as kerosene, gasoline, aviation fuel, diesel, and so on. This is because there were few, if any, refineries in Saudi Arabia. Crude goes out; as we've seen, that was the basis for the price, and it affects everything "downstream," such as refining. As they used to say down on the oil rig, "who'da thunk it?"

The solution to that problem also seemed straightforward: build refineries. A lot goes into that equation, such as forecast oil prices, location and logistics, and transportation infrastructure. They did need not park refineries on the Eastern Province coast when demand was countrywide. Quell surprise – that is exactly what has occurred. The Saudis have since built new refineries and have announced the goal of being the world's number two refiner by 2017.

And, last, a look at military threats and activity. No one, least of all those of us who have waged war in the desert, wants even a tenuous peace to be shattered. In the Middle East particularly and the world in general, the last war portends the next one, whether we want to accept it or not. We've discussed the fanatic threats of Houthi Shi'as and the IS. Neither, brutal as they are, will last forever. Syria continues to pose a profound challenge for U.S. foreign policy, but there is an equally if not more antagonistic threat. The United Nations, led by the United States and/or Israel, will very carefully monitor Iranian adherence to nuclear restrictions. While conciliatory, the fundamental Iranian view has not changed, save to prefer sanctions removed. Should Iranian enrichment via centrifuge resume or continue, conflict appears to be inevitable. Iran simply cannot be allowed to develop a nuclear weapon and delivery systems.

The US Navy and Air Force can keep the Straits of Hormuz secure, but while most of the rest of the world seeks nonproliferation and denuclearization, Iran sticks out like a sore and infected thumb. The United Nations, led by the United States and, of course, Israel, would act. And Iran is far too close for the Gulf Cooperation Council (a consortium of Arabian Peninsula Arab countries) not to be watching it carefully. We still should be concerned about terrorism and demand our leadership look to military leaders in force deployment decisions, but while we are concerned about shadowy terrorist groups who corrupt the intent and language of a major religion, strategically Iran is not going away.

The Saudis leading, moderate Arab states have clearly planted their mark in concern about Iran. The Nejd is threatened to the north by the IS, and has Iranian extremism nipping at its heels, but some of us are fans of the Nejd, in case it escaped your notice. Like the great, wild lands remaining on earth, the Nejd has thankfully not yielded to mere humans, however evil in their designs, enshallah.

Mysalaama.

# 10

# Acknowledgments

Substantially I am indebted to Colonel George K. Williams, Ph. D., for his unfailing friendship and perspective; to Christine Moss Helms, Ph.D., one of the finest Arabists I will ever meet; to Ambassador Oliver Miles of the United Kingdom, a Middle East diplomat and Oxford scholar who generously has shared his thoughts with me over now 15 years; to Stanley Alluisi, Ph.D., who was with me in the Nejd and, insistent on the title of the book (he is and now an intrepid scholar of things aeronautical); to Vahan Zanoyan, President of the Petroleum Finance Company, my professional host and personal friend; to Edward Morse for his concise tutelage and masterful insight into oil markets; to Ann McNary, for her assistance with graphics; to former Secretary of Defense William Cohen, himself a prolific author who allowed me to observe the craft of military diplomacy around the world; to General Charles Horner, USAF (ret.), a great commander for "stand-up" airmen; to Colonel Chris Christon, USAF (ret.), an air intelligence leader who took on the most daunting tasks with a cigar, guts, and capacious knowledge; to Colonel Bill Hubbard, USAF (ret.), my first squadron commander and a true font of leadership and encouragement; to the staff of the USAF Special Operations School for their insight; to the Council on Foreign Relations for access to some of the finest scholars in the world, and to CreateSpace, a wonderful conduit for once-and-future authors.

Particular recognition is due Lt. Gen. Erwin Rokke, USAF (ret.), PhD, for whom I worked throughout my air force career; Colonel Robert Haffa, USAF (ret.), PhD, who remains a mentor almost three decades after he swore me in as a USAF officer; and US Army Colonel Robert Young, a Middle East area specialist and Arabist who first taught me the complexities of the region during my undergraduate studies. *Shukran* (thank you) to them all.

Author in the Nejd south of Riyadh

www.ingramcontent.com/pod-product-compliance
Lightning Source LLC
Chambersburg PA
CBHW060228290526
45789CB00003B/1460